Anteaters

Victoria Blakemore

Copyright info/picture credits

Table of Contents

What Are Anteaters?

Anteaters are large mammals. They are known for their long snout and tongue. They are related to sloths and are sometimes called "ant bears."

There are three main kinds of anteaters. They differ in their size and where they live.

Most anteaters are gray in color,

with a long black and white

band of fur.

Size

The giant anteater is the largest anteater. It can be up to four feet long. Its tail can be up to three feet long. They can weigh up to 140 pounds.

Other anteaters are much smaller. They are usually less than two feet long and only weigh one or two pounds.

Male anteaters are usually

larger than female anteaters.

Physical Characteristics

Anteaters have a long, pointed snout. They use their snout to find food. Inside their snout is their long, sticky tongue.

They have long, sharp claws. They use them to protect themselves from predators such as jaguars.

Anteaters have a long, bushy tail. It can be used to give them shade from the sun.

Habitat

Anteaters live in rainforests, swamps, woodlands, and grasslands. Some are even found in mountainous areas.

They live in places where there are lots of insects. They are found in **climates** where it is usually warm.

Range

Anteaters are found in parts
Central and South America.

They are often seen in countries such as Brazil, Peru, Mexico, and Panama.

Diet

Anteaters are a special kind of **carnivore** called an **insectivore**. This means that they only eat insects.

Their diet is made up of insects such as ants and termites.

An anteater's tongue is **narrow** and sticky. It can be up to two feet long.

Anteaters do not have any teeth. Their stomach grinds up the insects that they eat.

They use their sharp claws to tear open an ant or termite mound. Then, they use their long, sticky tongue to collect the insects. They can eat about 30,000 in one day.

They often feed on an insect
mound for about one minute
before moving on to the next
mound.

Communication

Anteaters can use sound,

movement, and smell to

communicate.

Anteaters can hiss, grunt, snort,

and sniff to communicate.

Many of their sounds are used

as warnings to other animals

that may get too close.

Adult anteaters do not usually

vocalize. Young anteaters

make high-pitched squeals if

they are in danger.

Movement

Anteaters have a **unique** way of walking. Their claws curl up into their feet. This keeps their claws from wearing down.

They are usually slow-moving. They have been **observed** moving at speeds of eighteen miles per hour for short distances.

Silky anteaters are very good climbers. They spend a lot of their time in trees.

Anteater Pups

Anteaters usually have one baby, which is called a pup. A pup spends the first year riding on its mother's back.

Their fur blends in with their mother's fur, which provides them with **camouflage** from predators.

Young anteaters spend about
two years with their mother.
Then, they are able to take care
of themselves.

Anteater Life

Anteaters are **solitary**, which means that they spend most of their time alone.

Many anteaters are **nocturnal**. They are usually most active at night. Others may be more active during the morning and evening.

Many anteaters rest during the day, when it is the hottest. Some kinds of anteaters rest in trees.

Swimming Anteaters?

Giant anteaters are very good swimmers. They paddle with their legs and feet. Other kinds of anteaters can also swim.

When they are swimming, anteaters use their snout like a snorkel. They keep it out of the water so they can breathe.

Anteaters may swim to cross

rivers or lakes in their habitats.

Population

Giant anteaters are listed as **vulnerable**. Their populations have been **declining**. There are thought to be fewer than 5,000 giant anteaters left in the wild.

The population of silky anteaters that lives in Brazil is **critically endangered**. There are very few left.

In the wild, anteaters usually live

for about fourteen years.

Anteaters in Danger

Anteaters are facing several threats. The main threat to anteaters is habitat loss.

Many anteater habitats are being destroyed for farmland, buildings, and roads. This can make it difficult for anteaters to find enough food.

In some places, anteaters have

been hunted for their claws

and **hides**.

Helping Anteaters

In some places, special protected areas have been set up. These **preserves** provide animals like anteaters with a safe habitat.

Some groups are focused on fire prevention. Brushfires can be dangerous for animals like anteaters.

In parts of Argentina, anteaters that are born in **captivity** are taught to survive in the wild. Then, they are able to be released.

The goal of all of these programs is to help anteaters. People want to keep them from becoming **extinct**.

Glossary

Camouflage: using color to blend in to the surroundings

Captivity: animals that are kept by humans, not in the wild

Carnivore: an animal that eats only meat

Climate: the usual weather in a place

Critically Endangered: nearly extinct

Declining: getting smaller

Extinct: when there are no more of an animal left in the wild

Hides: animal skins

Insectivore: an animal that eats only insects

Narrow: not wide, thin

Nocturnal: animals that are active and night

Observed: seen

Preserves: areas of land set up to protect plants and animals

Solitary: living alone

Unique: special, different

Vocalize: to make sounds

Vulnerable: open to threat or harm, when an animal may become endangered

About the Author

Victoria Blakemore is a first grade

teacher in Southwest Florida with a

passion for reading.

You can visit her at

www.elementaryexplorers.com

Also in This Series

Gray Wolves	Sloths	Flamingos	Camels	Koalas	Honey Bees	Pandas
Pangolins	White-Tailed Deer	Orcas	Giraffes	Corn	Meerkats	Echidnas
Walruses	Raccoons	Bald Eagles	Apples	Arctic Foxes	Red Pandas	Cassowaries
Tigers	Ladybugs	Moose	Beluga Whales	Leopards	Elephants	Jellyfish
Binturongs	Lions	Dolphins	Reindeer	Hammerhead Sharks	Hippos	Pumpkins
Peafowl	Chameleons	Florida Panthers	Aye-Ayes	Black Bears	Cheetahs	Manatees
Gingerbread	Polar Bears	Hot Chocolate	Orangutans	Coyotes	Marshmallows	Strawberries

Also in This Series

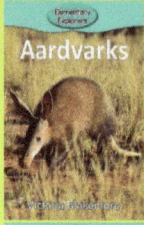

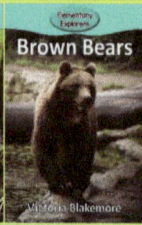

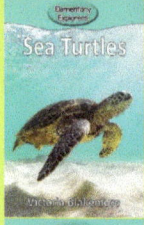

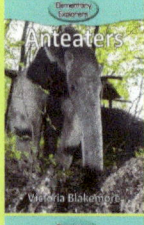

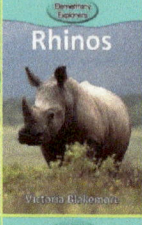

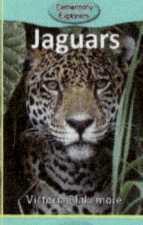

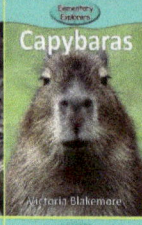

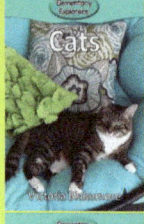

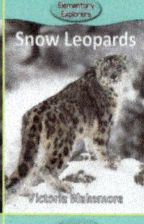

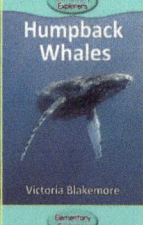

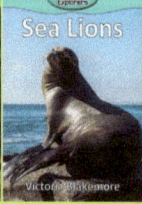

Aardvarks	Mako Sharks	Alligators	Frogs	Hedgehogs	Brown Bears	Bongos
Sea Turtles	Quokkas	Muskrats	Zebras	Red Foxes	Ring-Tailed Lemurs	Platypuses
Anteaters	Kangaroos	Rhinos	Jaguars	Wombats	Capybaras	Gorillas
Cats	Skunks	Butterflies	Dingoes	Snow Leopards	African Wild Dogs	Penguins
Whale Sharks	Wolverines	Warthogs	Caracals	Badgers	Seals	Hummingbirds
Pikas	Humpback Whales	Pumas	Lemonade	Llamas	Tulips	Ostriches
Sunflowers	Fennec Foxes	Sea Lions	Squirrels	Roses	Porcupines	Ice Cream

www.ingramcontent.com/pod-product-compliance
Lightning Source LLC
Chambersburg PA
CBHW051250020426
42333CB00025B/3143